REDUCE, REUSE, RECYCLE!

Food Waste

Deborah Chancellor

WAYLAND

First published in 2009 by Wayland

Copyright © Wayland 2009

Wayland
338 Euston Road
London NW1 3BH

Wayland Australia
Level 17/207 Kent Street
Sydney NSW 2000

Editor: Katie Powell
Designer: Elaine Wilkinson
Consultant: Kate Ruttle
Picture Researcher: Shelley Noronha
Photographer: Andy Crawford

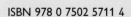

British Library Cataloguing in Publication Data

Chancellor, Deborah
Food waste. - (Reduce, reuse, recycle!)
1. Organic wastes - Juvenile literature 2. Organic wastes -
Recycling - Juvenile literature 3. Waste minimization -
Juvenile literature
I. Title
363.7'288

ISBN 978 0 7502 5711 4

Cover: © RecycleNow.

pg 1 Recycle Now, 2 Wayland, 4 Wayland, 5 Paul Hobson / naturepl.com; 6/7 Maria Teijeiro/Getty Images, 7(t) Emmanuel Faure/ Getty Images, 8 Wayland, 9 Recycle Now, 10 Wayland, 11 Peter Landon/Ecoscene, 12 National Geographic/Getty Images, 13 Khin Maung Win/AFP/Getty Images, 14 Recycle Now, 15 Recycle Now, 16 Wayland, 17 Paul Cowan/ISTOCK, 18 moodboard/Corbis, 20 Rolf Bruderer/Corbis, 21 Ricky John Molloy/Getty Images, 23 George Doyle/Getty Images, 24 Ian Garlick/ Getty Images, 25 Sally Morgan/Ecoscene, 26 Vicki Coombs/Ecoscene, 27 Sally Morgan/Ecoscene, 28/29 Wayland, Cover: Recycle Now.

With thanks to RecycleNow for kind permission to reproduce the photographs on the cover, title page, 9, 14, 15 and 22.

The author and publisher would like to thank the following models: Lawrence Do of Scotts Park Primary School, Sam Mears and Madhvi Paul.

Printed in China

Wayland is a division of Hachette Children's Books, an Hachette UK company.
www.hachettelivre.co.uk

Contents

Words in **bold** can be found in the glossary.

What is food waste?

All the food we do not eat becomes food waste. We throw away a lot of food every week. Some of it **rots** before we can eat it, or sometimes we just don't want it. Most food waste ends up in rubbish dumps called **landfill sites**.

◄ *In the United Kingdom (UK), a fifth of all rubbish in landfill sites is wasted food.*

When we throw food away it attracts pests, such as rats, foxes and flies. Pests can spread **germs** and make us ill. As food rots in landfill sites, it lets off harmful gases. These gases **pollute** the air and are bad for the **environment**.

▲ *The smell of food waste in bins attracts pests, such as this hungry rat.*

Did You Know?

Every year, 7 million tonnes of food are thrown away in the UK. 1.5 million elephants would weigh this much! Seven times more food is thrown away in the United States of America (USA).

What a waste!

We can all do something about food waste. **Reducing**, **reusing** and **recycling** our food helps deal with the problem. We can buy less food in the first place. We can also reuse food scraps by cooking another meal with them.

▼ *You can reuse fruit and vegetable scraps by feeding them to your pet.*

When you and your family go shopping, only buy what you actually need. This means less food and packaging will be wasted.

▲ Write a shopping list and stick to it in the shop.

YOU CAN HELP

1. Try to eat all your food at meal times, so there is no leftover food.

2. Avoid snacks. The packaging is often hard to recycle.

3. Put any food you can't eat into a separate bin so it can be recycled.

Shopping for food

Have you ever noticed the dates on food in shops? 'Sell-by' dates tell the shop when the food has to be sold by. 'Best-before' dates tell you how long the food will stay fresh and 'use-by' dates tell you when the food will start to go off.

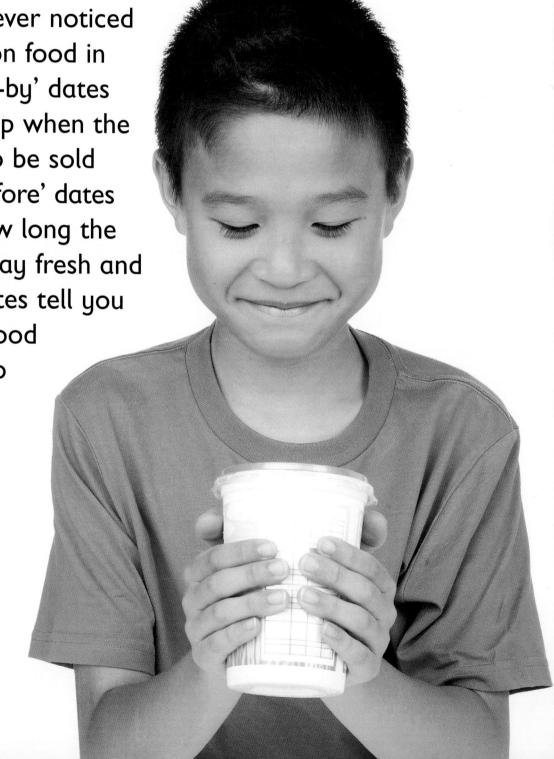

▶ *Food is not safe to eat if it has passed its 'use-by' date. Always check the date on the packaging.*

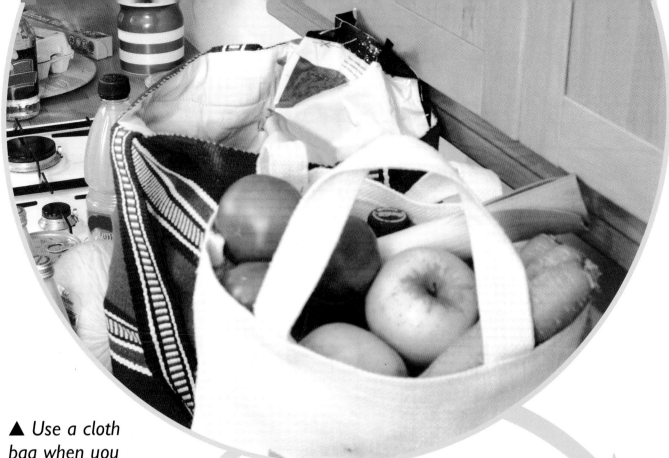

▲ Use a cloth bag when you go shopping, to save using a plastic one. The cloth bag can be reused.

We often waste food we buy, especially fruit, vegetables, meat and **dairy foods**. In the UK, the food we throw away in one year is enough to fill one out of three shopping bags. There are other kinds of waste linked to food, too. Food packaging and plastic bags make up a large amount of rubbish.

Food packaging

Most food is wrapped in packaging. When food is eaten, the packaging is no longer needed and ends up as waste. Instead it could be recycled at a **recycling centre** or collected by your **council** to be recycled.

▼Glass, aluminium, paper, cardboard and some plastics can be recycled.

It is best to buy food with as little packaging as possible, such as unwrapped fruit and vegetables. Ready-made food and takeaway meals are wrapped in lots of packaging, which often ends up as waste.

You Can Help!

Try to buy unpackaged food and ask your parents to buy big containers of food instead of small ones. This means you will waste less packaging.

▲ Most plastic packaging takes a long time to rot when it is dumped in landfill sites.

Factories, shops and restaurants

We waste lots of food at home, but food is wasted in other places as well. Food factories reject anything that is not perfect. Food is thrown away if the quality is not good enough for it to be sold in the shops, even though it is still fine to eat.

▼ *These chocolate chips will be thrown away if they are the wrong shape.*

Shops must sell food before it reaches its 'sell-by' date. They reduce the price of food when it is close to its 'sell-by' date, and afterwards, they take it off the shelves. Some supermarkets give this food away to help people in need, such as the homeless.

LOOKING AT 'SELL-BY' DATES

1. Which foods have short 'sell-by' dates?

2. Which foods have long 'sell-by' dates?

3. Try to eat the food that will go off first, so it is not wasted.

▲ **Food aid** is also given to people who have been affected by **natural disasters**. Some of the food comes from supermarkets.

Fruit and vegetables

Fruit and vegetables are fresh foods. They are wasted more than many other kinds of food because they rot very quickly. Every day in the UK, over 4 million apples, 5 million potatoes and nearly 2 million bananas end up in the bin.

▲ Choose fruit that is not quite ripe, so it lasts longer.

USING FRUIT

1. Ask an adult to help you chop up fruit and mix it with apple juice to make a fruit salad.

2. Blend ripe fruit with some milk or yoghurt to make a smoothie.

3. Ask an adult to help you cook soft fruits such as strawberries, raspberries and blackberries with sugar to make some jam.

Over-ripe fruit and vegetables can be reused instead of being thrown away. Vegetables can be made into soup, and fruit can be blended to make smoothies. Rotten fruit and vegetables can be recycled and put on a **compost heap** to make a natural **fertiliser** for the garden.

▶ *If fruit and vegetables do start to rot, don't throw them away. Put them on a compost heap.*

Meat and dairy foods

Meat and dairy foods must be kept in a **fridge** to stay fresh. If they are not kept cool, or if they are stored for too long, they will start to rot.

▼ *When milk goes off, it begins to smell, and must be thrown away.*

Keep an eye on the 'use-by' dates of meat and dairy foods. Remember that these foods go off more quickly in hot weather. If you think some meat is close to its 'use-by' date, ask an adult to cook a meal with it. The meal can always be **frozen** to eat on another day.

▶ *This shepherd's pie is an ideal meal to be frozen to eat another day.*

Did You Know?

Every day in the UK, more than 1 million pots of yoghurt are wasted because they have gone past their 'sell-by' date. They aren't even opened before they are thrown in the bin.

Keep it fresh

Fresh food tastes good. Fresh vegetables and fruit have lots of **vitamins** and **minerals** in them, which help to keep us healthy. The fresher our food is, the better it is for us. Unfortunately, we waste lots of fresh food because we do not eat it before it goes off.

▼ *Always eat the ripest piece of fruit in the bowl. It may not keep until tomorrow.*

Food often needs to be kept cool and can be chilled in the fridge. Most food can also be frozen to keep it fresh. Food tastes better if it is not frozen for too long. Some food freezes very well, for example **raw** meat and fish.

▲ Keep food and drink that needs to be chilled in the fridge.

USEFUL TIPS

1. Store foods separately in containers with lids.

2. If you spot any mouldy food, remove it straight away because it will make the rest of your food go off more quickly.

3. Don't store fruit and vegetables in plastic bags or they will quickly start to rot.

19

Local and seasonal food

We can buy food out of season because it has been **transported** to this country by plane or road. But this uses lots of **energy**. It is better to eat food that is grown locally. It is fresher, and less energy has been used to move it around. Less traffic **pollution** has been made on the food's journey, too.

◀ *Try to find shops and markets near your home that sell local food. If you can, pick your own fruit at a farm.*

You could even grow your own food. Some fruits and vegetables, such as carrots, lettuces and tomatoes, are easy to grow. There are no transport and packaging costs, so it saves energy and reduces pollution, which is good for the environment.

◀ If you have a garden, you could turn part of it into vegetable patch.

Reducing food waste

We can all help to reduce the amount of food we waste. Ask your parent to plan family meals for a week, and only buy what they need. Check the 'use-by' dates on food, and make sure you can eat it in time, or that you can freeze it.

▲ 'Buy-one-get-one-free' offers are good value, but will your family eat it all?

Did YOU KnOW?

Over half of all food dumped in landfill sites is untouched — which means it was probably not really needed in the first place.

▲ *Ready-made meals are very wasteful because they are wrapped in a lot of packaging.*

Ready-made meals have lots of packaging, and food and energy is wasted making them in factories. Ask your parent to buy fresh ingredients with little or no packaging, and follow a recipe to cook a meal. This will cut down on food and packaging waste.

Reusing food waste

In the past people did not waste as much food as they do today. There was less food available to eat, so it was not thrown away. Instead of ending up in the bin, leftovers were often reused to make new meals.

▲ 'Bubble and squeak' is a meal made from leftover fried vegetables.

COOKING LEFTOVERS

1. Add ripe bananas and yoghurt to pancake mixture, to make pancakes.

2. Fry cooked rice and vegetables with eggs and onions, to make egg fried rice.

3. Boil leftover roast vegetables with some stock to make soup.

4. Use leftover meat to make a curry.

◀ *Some recycling centres collect waste oil. It can be reused to make soap, make-up and skin creams.*

Some kinds of food waste can be used again instead of being thrown away. Cooking oil, for example, can be reused a few times. You should not throw old cooking oil down the sink because it can block pipes.

Recycling food waste

No matter how hard you try to reduce and reuse food waste, there is always going to be some. Put any food waste into a separate bin, so it can be collected from your home.

▼ In many countries, food waste is collected from bins outside people's homes.

You can recycle food waste on a compost heap. The food **breaks down** to make fertiliser for your garden. Fruit and vegetable peelings, tea bags, coffee grounds and eggshells rot well on a compost heap. Don't add meat, eggs, or dairy foods to your compost heap because they attract pests.

◀ *Small tiger worms are kept in some compost bins called* **wormeries**. *They are very fast at breaking down food waste.*

Did You Know?

In the UK, only about 4 per cent of food waste ends up as compost. In the US, just 7 per cent of food waste is recycled in this way.

Make a smoothie

Smoothies are delicious fruity drinks. They are also good for you because the fruit in them has lots of vitamins and minerals. Making smoothies is a great way to use ripe fruit.

YOU WILL NEED:

- a blender,
- 6 strawberries,
- 1 banana,
- 1 teaspoon of honey,
- 150ml (5 fl oz) natural yoghurt or milk,
- a measuring jug,
- a knife,
- a glass and straw,
- a chopping board.

1. Wash the strawberries and take off the leaves and stalks.

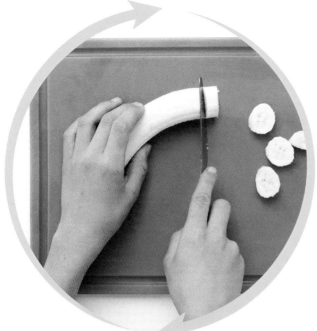

2. Peel and cut up the banana.

3. Measure out the yoghurt or milk in a measuring jug. Add the honey.

4. Put all the ingredients in a blender and mix them together.

5. Pour the mixture into a glass and enjoy your smoothie!

Further information

Topic map

SCIENCE

Leave some potatoes in a sealed plastic bag for a week. They will let off gas inside the bag, and begin to rot.

MATHS

Look at the 'sell-by' dates on some packaging. Put them in order, from the closest date to the date that is furthest away.

ENGLISH

Imagine you are a banana! Tell the story of your life, from growing on a banana plant to being made into a smoothie.

GEOGRAPHY

Look at labels on some fruit to see where it comes from. Find that place or country on an atlas. How far away is it?

DESIGN

Use food packaging to do some junk modelling. Make a robot, using cardboard boxes, foil cartons and plastic bottle tops.

PSHE

Find out about healthy eating, and why it is important to eat fresh food.

Further reading

Dealing with Waste: Leftover Food by Sally Hewitt (Franklin Watts, 2006)

Environment Action: Recycle by Kay Barnham (Wayland, 2008)

Green Team: Your Food by Sally Hewitt (Franklin Watts, 2008)

Improving Our Environment: Waste and Recycling by Carol Inskipp (Wayland, 2005)

Re-using and Recycling by Ruth Thomson (Franklin Watts, 2006)

Websites

www.olliesworld.com
Children's website with information on recycling in USA, Australia and UK.

www.recyclingconsortium.org.uk/primary/info/menu.htm
Information for children on the 3 R's.

www.bbc.co.uk/gardening/gardening_with_children/
homegrownprojects_compost.shtml
Tips on how to set up your own compost heap.

www.lovefoodhatewaste.com
Ideas on what to do with leftover food.

www.epa.gov/kids
Information for children on recycling and dealing with waste in the USA.

www.sgaonline.org.au
Information and tips on vegetable gardening in Australia.

Glossary

breaks down to decay or rot

compost heap a rotten mix of leaves, plants and grass

council the organisation that runs services in your area

dairy food a kind of food made from milk

energy the power to do work

environment the world around us, and all living things

fertiliser a substance added to soil to make plants grow more easily

food aid food given to those in need

fridge a metal cupboard where food is kept cool and fresh

frozen to keep things below freezing temperature

germ a very tiny living thing that can make you ill

landfill site a rubbish dump, where waste is buried underground

mineral a natural substance that is an important part of a healthy diet

natural disaster an extreme event of nature, for example a hurricane

pollute to make something dirty

pollution dirt in the air, water or earth

raw food that is not cooked

recycle when something is made into a new product

recycling centre a place where you take things to be recycled

reduce to make something smaller or use less of it

reuse when something is used again

rot when a substance breaks down

transport to move from one place to another

vitamin a substance in food that you need to stay fit and well

wormery a composter that uses worms to break down food waste

Index

Numbers in **bold** refer to a photograph.